TIMELESS
CHINA

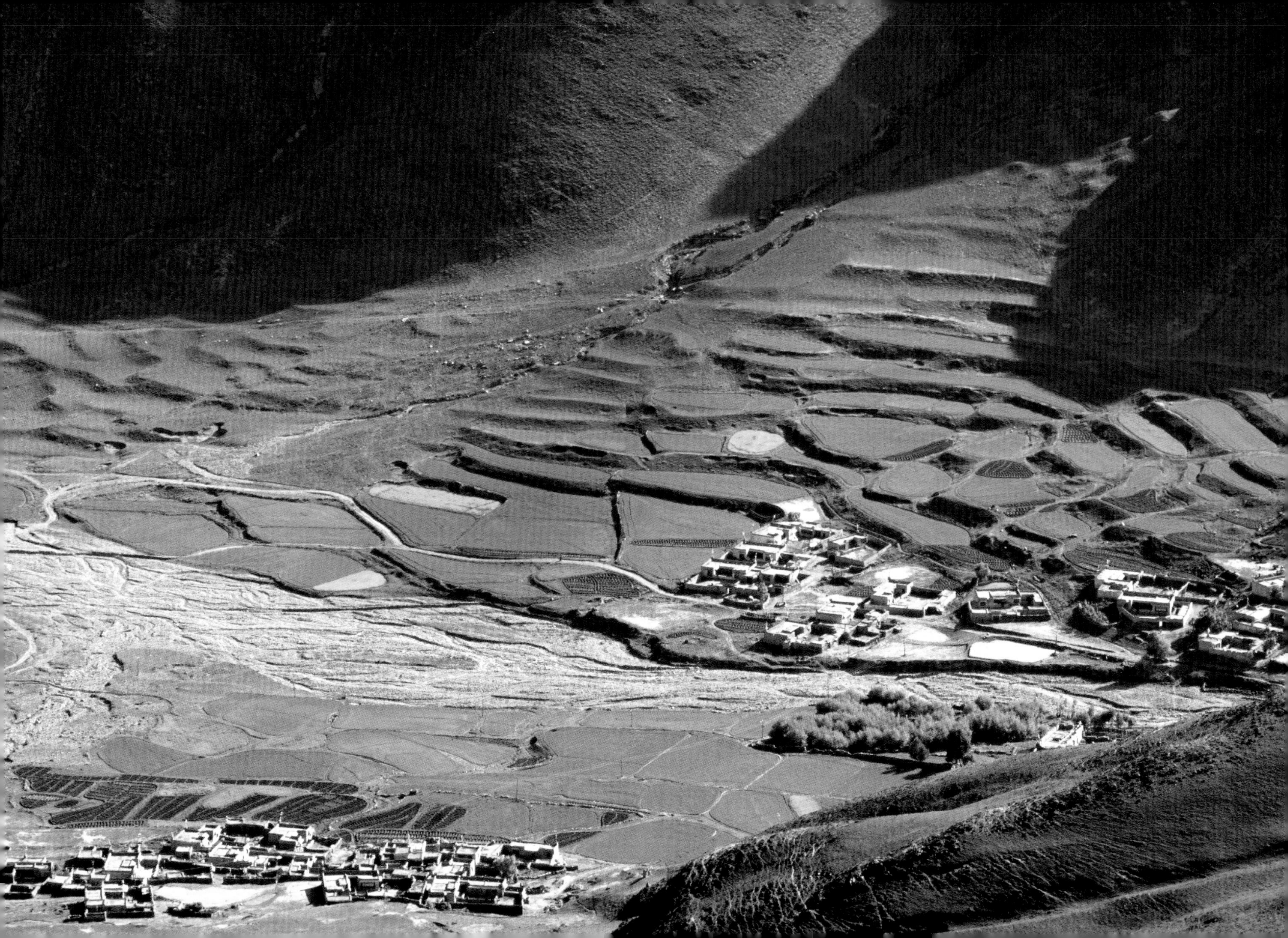

TIMELESS
CHINA

Ian Westwell

CHARTWELL
BOOKS, INC.

This edition published in 2007 by

CHARTWELL BOOKS, INC.
A Division of
BOOK SALES, INC.
114 Northfield Avenue
Edison, New Jersey 08837

ISBN-13: 978-0-7858-2318-6
ISBN-10: 0-7858-2318-2

© 2007 Compendium Publishing, 43 Frith Street,
London, Soho, W1V 4SA, United Kingdom

Cataloging-in-Publication data is available from the
Library of Congress

All rights reserved. No part of this publication may be
reproduced, stored in a retrieval system or transmitted in
any form or by any means, electronic, mechanical,
photocopying, recording or otherwise, without the prior
permission of Compendium Publishing Ltd. All correspon-
dence concerning the content of this volume should be
addressed to Compendium Publishing Ltd

Printed and bound in Hong Kong

Design: Compendium Design

PAGE 2: Until recently, China has been a largely rural
society. Now, increasingly, it has become the indudtrial
powerhouse of the world.

PAGE 4: Shanghai's Bund has been a cosmopolitan
meeting ground between east and west since the 19th
century. This picture shows the former Shanghai
International Settlement: for a modern view of this area
see pages 148–149.

Contents

Introduction

Introduction

China has a land area of some 3.7 million sq miles, making it the third largest country on Earth behind Russia and Canada, but around 90 percent of its population, the world's largest at more than one billion, is actually found in just 50 percent of its total area.

The geography of China

As befits a country that stretches something like 3,000 miles from north to south and is 3,200 miles east to west at its maximum extent, China's geography is diverse and has had a decisive impact on the country's population distribution. Something like 65 percent of its area is either mountain, desert or otherwise unsuitable for human habitation. Overall the land falls away from west to east, from the high ground of the western provinces to the river basins of the east. The high ground of the southwest consists of a series of high plateaux that reach up to 14,750 feet above sea level and to the south of these lies the easternmost extension of the world's greatest mountain range, the Himalayas.

Both these peaks and plateaux provide the melt water that fuels many of China's great rivers, including the Yangtze and Yellow. The former is the

PREVIOUS PAGE: Misty mountains in Anhui Province. Located in east China, the south of the province is dominated by the Yangtze.

RIGHT: Rapeseed fields in Yunnan Province, in southwest China. Yunnan means "south of the clouds," and it shares a border with Tibet, Myanmar, Laos, and Vietnam.

country's longest at 3,900 miles and its drainage basin covers close to 775,000 sq miles, roughly one fifth of the China's entire area and home to 400 million people. To the north of the peaks and plateau lies the largest arid area in China, the Taklamakan Desert. Farther eastward the high and arid ground gives way to the plains through which the Yangtze flows as well as similar flatlands to its north and east.

The people of China

China is the most populous nation on the planet and is still growing at a rate of between 8 and 10 million per year despite the adoption of the controversial one-child per family policy in the late 1970s. Demographers calculate that the country's population will continue to rise for the next few decades and zero-population growth might only be achieved by the 2030s. This population increase has also produced an imbalance between the sexes with 100 girls being born to every 117 boys, and the decline in fertility since the enactment of the one-child policy has led to an aging population. As of 2003 something like 10 percent of Chinese were over 60 and this is likely to increase to around 16 percent by 2020. Life expectancy is 70.4 years for men and 73.7 for women

China is one of the most ethnically diverse nations on Earth with as many as 56 different groups. Han Chinese, who are mostly found along the Pearl, Yangtze, and Yellow rivers, make up the overwhelming majority of the population (92 percent), while the other 55 groups, known as "national minorities" and numbering around 100 million people, are largely found along the borderlands stretching in an arc from the southwest to the northeast. Yunnan in the far southwest is the most ethnically diverse province in China and is home to 20 different groups. With a population of 42 million, it contains roughly 35 percent of all the national minorities and just 50 percent of the total are Han Chinese.

The Chinese speak a wide variety of languages with a sizeable number of dialects and subdialects. The official language is what in the west in called Mandarin but in China is called putonghua (common speech) and is variously referred to as hanyu (Han language), guoyu (the national language) or zhongwen (Chinese). Mandarin is commonly spoken everywhere with the

exception of provinces in the west and southwest, where many of the national minority languages are found. Aside from putonghua there are seven other major groups of dialects, including yue (Cantonese) and wu (Shanghainese).

The Chinese practice many forms of religious observation but precise numbers are difficult to come by because many people have kept their beliefs private not least because the state has for a long time merely tolerated and not promoted such beliefs. It was not until 1982, for example, that the country's constitution was modified to allow freedom of worship. The best estimates suggest that there are 100 million Buddhists, 18 million Muslims, 10 million Protestants and 4 million Catholics. Despite these seemingly low figures, most other Chinese regularly take part in religion-type ceremonial events that have their origins in philosophies such as Confucianism and Taoism.

Politics and personal liberty

A few years after coming to power, the Chinese Communist Party divided the country into 21 provinces, five autonomous regions and made Beijing and Shanghai into municipalities. The Communist Party continues to dominate the country's political life, although there are a number of so-called Democratic Parties that have an advisory role. Communist Party membership stands at around 58 million people who are associated with some 3.3 million party branches across the country. Supreme power resides with the Central People's government and it operates through a vast bureaucracy of ministries and provincial governments. Corruption, especially at lower official levels in rural areas, remains a significant problem, and there has been a traditional reluctance to investigate official incompetence or mismanagement.

While recent governments have followed a path of economic liberalism, personal freedom is tightly controlled especially access to international media

LEFT: Jing Jing, a panda who was chosen as one of the Olympic mascots, plays at the Chengdu Research Base of Giant Panda Breeding.

like the internet. There are thousands of home-grown newspapers and even more periodicals available to read but many are either state-controlled like the *People's Daily* or closely monitored in what they print. Individual or group displays of non-conformity or dissent are also likely to be dealt with severely as the events at Beijing's Tiananmen Square in 1989 testified. The country's legal system is likely to need a major overhaul and the country regularly uses the death penalty despite frequent condemnation. At an international level China still has ongoing territorial disputes with both India and Japan, and its occupation of Tibet since 1950 has been widely and repeatedly condemned. China is slowly opening itself up to the wider world (and possibly its influences) as the 2008 Olympic Games indicates but whether this is followed by a bout of social liberalization remains a moot point.

China's booming economy

After an initial post-civil war period of wide-ranging economic reform that seemed to promise much, the Chinese economy largely stagnated for more than two decades after the creation of the People's Republic of China in 1949. Indeed, it was often mismanaged with calamitous results. This was most evident in the Great Leap Forward of 1958–1960, a hugely ambitious plan to fully modernize certain of the country's industries. It proved a costly failure that brought about a famine that killed 30 to 60 million Chinese and led Mao Zedong to resign as head of state but not his chairmanship of the Communist Party.

The roots of the post-Mao boom stretch back to the re-election of modernizer Deng Xiaoping in the late 1970s. He developed the so-called Four Modernizations in which agriculture, defence, industry, and science were to be overhauled. During the next decade, the central government also established

RIGHT: Mt. Tianzi is well known for its mists and clouds.

FAR RIGHT: Maps showing the growth of China.

GROWTH OF CHINA
1350 BC TO TODAY

- 1359 BC
- AD 200 HAN DYNASTY
- 1227 MONGOL EMPIRE
- 1780
- 1936

— · — INTERNATIONAL BORDERS

- - - DISPUTED BORDERS

○ CAPITAL CITIES

○ MAJOR CITIES

1936 MONGOLIA CEDED

1950 TIBET INVADED

DISPUTED TERRITORIES

PRC TODAY

liberalized business and trading areas, known as Special Economic Zones, along the coast in which initially state owned—but increasingly privately owned free-market businesses—were allowed to flourish. The return of Hong Kong in 1997 also gave China control one of the world's most important financial centers. The countryside also felt the wind of change but to a lesser degree when farmers were allowed to sell of surplus produce for personal profit under a measure known as the Responsibility System.

This economic miracle is being bought about at a price and China is set to become the world's biggest polluter in the near future. The chief culprit is coal, which currently generates some 70 percent of the country's power needs and requires the burning of 900 million tons per annum. Aside from the smog this produces and which hangs over many of China's major cities, scientists estimate that 30 percent of the country receives excessive levels of acid rain. The latter has had a devastating effect on the already poor quality of the country's rivers which are routinely used as sewers and is having a seriously detrimental impact on its (and its neighbor's) forestry. There is some evidence that China is beginning to address these problems but there is still a long way to go as the government largely puts the economy above the environment.

Economic expansion has had a human cost. The country's urban population stands at more than 40 percent of the total and rising, a situation that is placing a huge strain on infrastructure, including water supply and waste disposal. The fruits of the boom are very unevenly distributed. There is already a gap between the incomes of urban dwellers and peasant farmers, many of whom operate at subsistence level, of around three percent and there is no

LEFT: Bamboo is a much-used commodity over all of South Asia, here during the first stages of a bridge over the Yangtze.

FAR LEFT: In the background the Jade Mountain; in the foreground, the Yangtze—China's longest river and the world's third longest at 3,602 miles.

ABOVE: The first national forest park in China, Wulingyuan in Hunan is one of China's 33 world heritage sites.

LEFT: China's massive industrialization is powered by fossil fuels—much to the chagrin of the western green movement.

evidence that the disparity is disappearing. Equally, city dwellers enjoy subsidized welfare and healthcare, while those in rural areas do not. This inequality has also result in mass-migration by the rural poor into the big cities in search of higher wages but what they often find are poorly paid jobs in often dangerous conditions. This urban influx and overcrowding has become so great that the authorities have resorted to building new cities from scratch to alleviate the problem. The friction between urban and rural dwellers is not going to disappear that easily.

LEFT: A UNESCO World Heritage Site in Anhui Province, the Huangshan mountain range has 77 peaks over 3,000ft.

BELOW: Crescent Moon Lake Oasis in the Gobi Desert—Asia's largest desert.

ABOVE, RIGHT, AND FAR RIGHT:
Zhoukoudian is where Peking Man (*Homo erectus*) was discovered. A cave system near Beijing in China, the earliest remains were over 500,000 years old. In total some 40 bodies were found as well as animal remains and stone tools. It has been a world heritage site since 1987.

ABOVE: Under British rule from 1842 until it was returned to the People's Republic of China in 1997, Hong Kong is one of the wealthiest cities in the world—in 2006, its per-capita GDP was the sixth highest in the world.

RIGHT: Rice is the world's largest crop and it has been cultivated in China since 5000 B.C.

FAR RIGHT: The Yangtze is often called the "Golden Waterway" and carries a lot of commercial traffic.

22

LEFT: The Great Wall of China is not one but many walls, that have been built, destroyed, and rebuilt between the 5th century B.C. and the 16th century. Designed to protect the Chinese Empire's northern borders, it was an effective barrier—for example, it held the Manchus off for nearly 50 years until they were able to breach the wall by treachery and depose the Ming Dynasty.

RIGHT: The Potala Palace in Lhasa is now a state museum, a tourist attraction, and—of course—a UNESCO World Heritage Site. It was the palace of the Dalai Lamas before they were displaced by the Chinese.

Early Civilizations: 6000 B.C.–A.D. 420

Measuring approximately 4,000 miles from end to end, the Great Wall of China is the longest structure in the world. Roughly following the southern border of Inner Mongolia, it stretches from Shanhai Pass in the east to Lop Nur in the west.

Early Civilizations: 6000 B.C.–A.D. 420

Archaeologists in China have found evidence of a settled agricultural community dating back to around 6000 B.C. at Banpo and a second, known as the Langshan Culture, showing evidence of the metal working that probably produced the Shang Dynasty in the Bronze Age. The Shang emerged around 1700 B.C. and their empire gradually spread over much of northern China. Aside from establishing cities with defensive walls, the Shang developed a social structure based on kings, officials, soldiers, and peasants as well as metal workers who produced bronze artefacts.

The Shang were defeated in battle by the Zhou, a people from what is now east-central China, in around 1100 B.C. and the Zhou went on to establish a large empire. They first made their capital at Hao near Xi'an but later moved it to Luoyang so historians have divided the dynasty into the Western Zhou (1100 B.C.–771 B.C.) and the Eastern Zhou (770 B.C.–221 B.C.). The Zhou developed a legal system, began to work with iron, and saw the emergence of a wealthy middle class of merchants and administrators. However, the system of government in which lords ruled over various regions led to a 250-year period of instability known as the era of Warring States.

RIGHT: The Army of Terracotta Warriors of Shaanxi was a major world discovery when the underground vaults were first explored in 1974. Excavations eventually yielded thousands of life-size terracotta soldiers and their horses in battle formation. The warriors are over 2,000 years old and amazingly well preserved.

FAR RIGHT: Between Zhong and Peling on the Yangtze River is China's only "ghost town"—Fengdu. Surrounding the famous Mount Mingshan are Buddhist and Taoist temples complete with carvings and statues depicting hell and its inhabitants dating back 1,800 years. A popular tourist attraction, it only escaped submersion after construction of the Three Gorges Dam due to its lofty location.

The last of the leaders of the Warring States was overcome by the Qin people in 221 B.C. Their leader, Qin Shi Huang, took a hard line on crime and punishment and was also an empire builder, undertaking campaigns as far afield as Korea and Vietnam. Aside from building infrastructure and introducing standardized currency, the emperor began to create the Great Wall. The next Qin emperor was seen as weak and he was overthrown by a commoner, Liu Bang, in 207 B.C., and he founded the Han Dynasty.

The Han brought greater integration to the empire by incorporating states on the margins of their lands, especially during the reign of Emperor Wu (140 B.C.–87 B.C.). He took control of areas to the north and west of the empire and also introduced an examination system for potential government officials. The expansion of the empire led the Han to establish extensive trading links, most notably along the Silk Road that passed through Central Asia and carried on to Europe.

The Han ruled until A.D. 220 but because of the short-lived Xin Dynasty (A.D. 9–23), they are divided into the Western Han (206 B.C.–A.D. 9) and the Eastern Han (A.D. 25–220). The collapse of their dynasty and the empire saw China enter a prolonged period of disunity in which kingdoms rose and fell. The first of these were the Three Kingdoms of the Wei, Shu, and Wu (A.D. 220–280) and the Jin Dynasty (A.D. 265–420) but even after their latter's demise China faced close to 200 years of further upheaval.

PAGE 32: Huangshan Mountain in east China's Anhui Province offers some of the nation's most beautiful scenery. Its peaks— 77 of which are over 3,000 feet—are characterized by unusual rock formations, twisted pine trees, and clear springs.

RIGHT, FAR RIGHT, AND PAGE 33: In all, the Terracotta Army now numbers 8,099 warriors and horses who guard the mausoleum of Qin Shi Huangdi, the first Emperor of Qin who reigned as the first emperor of a unified China from 221 to 210 B.C., having been king of Qin Province from 247 to 221 B.C. It is thought that the life-size figures were constructed on an early "production line" system, with different parts being fired separately and then assembled. Despite this, each face is individual and the figures also have various uniforms, hairstyles, and heights according to their rank. When newly crafted they would have been colored to appear lifelike and carried real weapons and armor.

LEFT: This aerial photograph gives some impression of the incredible engineering feat undertaken by the Chinese over 2,000 years ago. Begun by order of Emperor Qin Shi Huang, the Great Wall was intended to join fortifications along his new empire's northern borders and give protection against incursions by the Xiongnu peoples.

LEFT: Initially built of whatever materials were locally available along its length, the wall today owes its appearance mostly to rebuilding work that took place during the Ming Dynasty (1368–1644) in order to keep the Mongols out of China.

ABOVE: The Ming builders crafted a wall that was larger and stronger than its predecessor, being made of brick and stone rather than the rammed earth and wood that characterized the earlier wall in regions where stone was not easily available.

PAGES 38 AND 39: Along the length of the wall are watchtowers—of vital importance as storehouses for weapons and food as well as providing barracks for those manning the wall. They also provided an efficient communication system over great distances.

ABOVE: Nanjing's Confucius Temple (also known as Fuzimiao) was originally built in 1034, but has been rebuilt on numerous occasions, most recently in 1984. Outside stands the nation's largest statue of Confucius, in bronze.

BELOW: The town of Qufu in Shandong Province was the hometown of Confucius and is now a UNESCO World Heritage Site. The philosopher and educator was born here in 551 B.C., and after his death in 479 B.C., his former home was consecrated as a temple. To the north of the town is the Cemetery of Confucius, where his original tomb was located and which now holds 3,600 tombstones, including those of his descendents as well as additional memorials to Confucius himself.

ABOVE, RIGHT, AND FAR RIGHT: Before the arrival of Buddhism in the first century A.D., the development of Chinese art and architecture was highly influenced by mythology and then Confucius. Over the centuries, art became highly appreciated, particularly in court circles, and Chinese painting, carving, and calligraphy became increasingly elaborate.

PAGES 44 AND 45: Restored, rebuilt, and added to over the centuries since Confucius' death, the temple in Qufu is now a sprawling historical complex second only in size to the Forbidden City.

FAR LEFT: A close-up photograph of the statue of Confucius that stands outside the Confucius Temple in Nanjing. Within the temple are a number of superb panels made of jade, gold, and silver, which detail the life of China's great philosopher.

LEFT: Another of China's great Confucian Temples is Kongmiao in Beijing. Built in 1302, the vast compound (second only in size to that at Qufu) contains numerous artefacts of historical and architectural interest including 198 steles which name all of the Confucian scholars who studied here between 1416 and 1904, as well as this ancient bell.

From Division to Unity: A.D. 420–907

The divisions that had seen China split into several competing kingdoms that had begun with the collapse of the Han Dynasty in A.D. 220 continued into the period known as the Northern and Southern Dynasties. It was an era of mostly short-lived dynasties that lasted between 420 and 589, and as the names suggest, there was a strong division between the north and south of China. There were four identifiable dynasties in the south—the Song (420–479), the Qi (479–502), the Liang (502–557), and the Chen (557–589)—and all had their capital at Nanjing. There were five Northern Dynasties: these were the Northern Wei (386–534), the Eastern Wei (534–550), the Northern Qui (550–557), the Western Wei (535–556), and the Northern Zhou (557–581). These had their capital in various locations, including Datong, Luoyang, Linzhang, and Xi'an.

While the somewhat more stable south enjoyed something of an economic boom, the north saw frequent bouts of warfare. The people of the north were also ruled over by non-Chinese monarchs and many of them fled during the unrest thereby taking Chinese culture and values into previously non-Chinese regions. The most successful of the Northern Dynasties was that of the Northern Wei, which was founded by the Buddhist Touba people. They

RIGHT: Artwork in the Mogao Caves, which would have originally been used by the monks who dwelled here as a meditation aid. The caves did not reveal their full treasure until around 1900 when their guardian, Wang Yuan-lu discovered a walled up cave that contained a trove of art and manuscripts dating between 406 and 1002.

FAR RIGHT: The Mogao Caves are set into desert cliffs above a river valley in Gansu. Some 492 grottoes still stand and they contain religious art depicting 1,000 years of history.

were renowned for the cave temples and also undertook land reform in rural areas and reorganized the administration of their capital. The age of division came to an end in 581 when a nobleman, Yang Jian, seized power and established the Sui Dynasty. Although the dynasty lasted little more than 35 years, it proved a milestone in Chinese history, not least because the north and south were reunited. The Sui's greatest contribution was the creation of the Grand Canal that linked the lower Yangtze River with Chang'an. The regime collapsed thanks to the military adventurism of Yang Jian's dissolute son, Sui Yangdi. He made three disastrous attacks on Korea that led to popular unrest against him and he was assassinated by one of his court officials in 618.

Sui Yangdi was replaced by Li Yuan, one of his foremost military commanders and founder of the Tang Dynasty. He spent the first decade of his rule elimination rivals and he then reorganized the administration of his empire to prevent regionalism. The Tang greatly expanded the empire, established trade routes with the Mediterranean by way of India and Persia (Iran) and welcomed foreign merchants on to Chinese soil. While many scholars see this as a golden era in Chinese history, the dynasty fell apart during the 8th and 9th centuries. There were threats to its northern and southern borders and heavy taxes help foment unrest in the Tang heartland that lead to the Huang Chao rebellion (874–884). The Tang empire began to fragment and the fall of their capital in 907 signaled the end of the dynasty.

RIGHT: Jiangxi's Lushan National Park is a stunningly beautiful area of mountains, lakes, springs, grottoes, and pools and is rich in historical interest. A center of Chinese civilization, the region abounds with temples, and has long attracted painters, poets and writers who have lauded its tranquil beauty.

FAR RIGHT: Mount Lushan encompasses more than 90 peaks, including the highest, Hanyang Feng at 4,836 feet. Often swathed in mist, the slopes of the mountain have yielded archeological finds dating back to the Ice Age.

LEFT: Serving as the westernmost fort of the early Tang Dynasty, Dunhuang was not only a key trading post situated on the "Silk Road," but became an important center of Buddhism. Foreign monks and their Chinese disciples formed the earliest Buddhist communities at Dunhuang in the late 3rd and early 4th centuries. Although it was only a small oasis town located in the desert of northwestern China, Dunhuang grew into the site of the largest complex of ancient Chinese art, including the Mogao Caves, which are located in the Gobi Desert a few miles away from the city.

RIGHT: As well as great natural beauty, numerous sites of historic interest can be found around Mount Lushan, including botanical gardens, the Academy of White Deer Cave, one of China's oldest seats of Confucian learning and Lulin Villa, a former home of Mao Zedong.

LEFT AND ABOVE: Now listed as a UNESCO World Heritage Site, carving of the Longmen Grottoes in Henan Province began somewhere around the year 493 and continued for 400 years. Roughly 30 percent of the caves have been dated to the Northern Wei Dynasty (368–534) and 60 percent to the Tang Dynasty (618–907).

PAGE 58: The most imposing statue on the Longmen site is the Vairacana Buddha, which sits cross-legged and measures over 56 feet in height. Records show that the mysterious Empress Wu Zetian (624–649) would have taken part in the Introducing the Light ceremony.

PAGE 59, LEFT AND RIGHT: The Longmen Caves Research Institute report that alongside 43 pagodas and 2,800 inscriptions the complex of caves and niches contains over 100,000 statues, almost all of which have a Buddhist theme.

RIGHT AND FAR RIGHT: In Sichuan Province, at the confluence of the Minjiang Dadu and Qingyi rivers, is the Leshan Buddha. Carved out of the rock of the cliff face, at almost 233 feet high it is the tallest stone sculpture of Buddha anywhere in the world and dates back to 713 when work commenced under the supervision of a monk called Haitong. It was carved in the belief that the deity would pacify the river beneath and protect shipping. In fact, the depositing of stone taken from the cliff during the 90 year project did much to alter the flow of the waters and helped make the river safer for traffic.

ABOVE AND RIGHT: The carving represents a Maitreya Buddha seated with hands on knees. Having suffered from centuries of erosion the Buddha is currently being restored, but remains a popular tourist draw set in parkland. Visitors are able to walk down the Nine Turn Cliff Road, which was carved into the cliff alongside the figure during the 8th century.

ABOVE: As with the Longmen and Mogao cave systems, the Yungang Caves, west of Datong in Shanxi Province, contain superbly crafted and preserved Buddhist sculpture. Built between 460 and 494 A.D., the wealth of statuary was carved from the rock and is some of the most ancient and important in China.

RIGHT AND FAR RIGHT: The Yungang Caves pierce the north cliff of Wuzhou Mountain and represent the Chinese belief that the emperor was Buddha as five of the statues depict the emperors Taizu, Taizong, Shizu, Gaozong, and Gaozu. The sculpture also shows the influence of Indian Buddhist art on that of traditional China.

From Five Dynasties to the Yuan: 907–1368

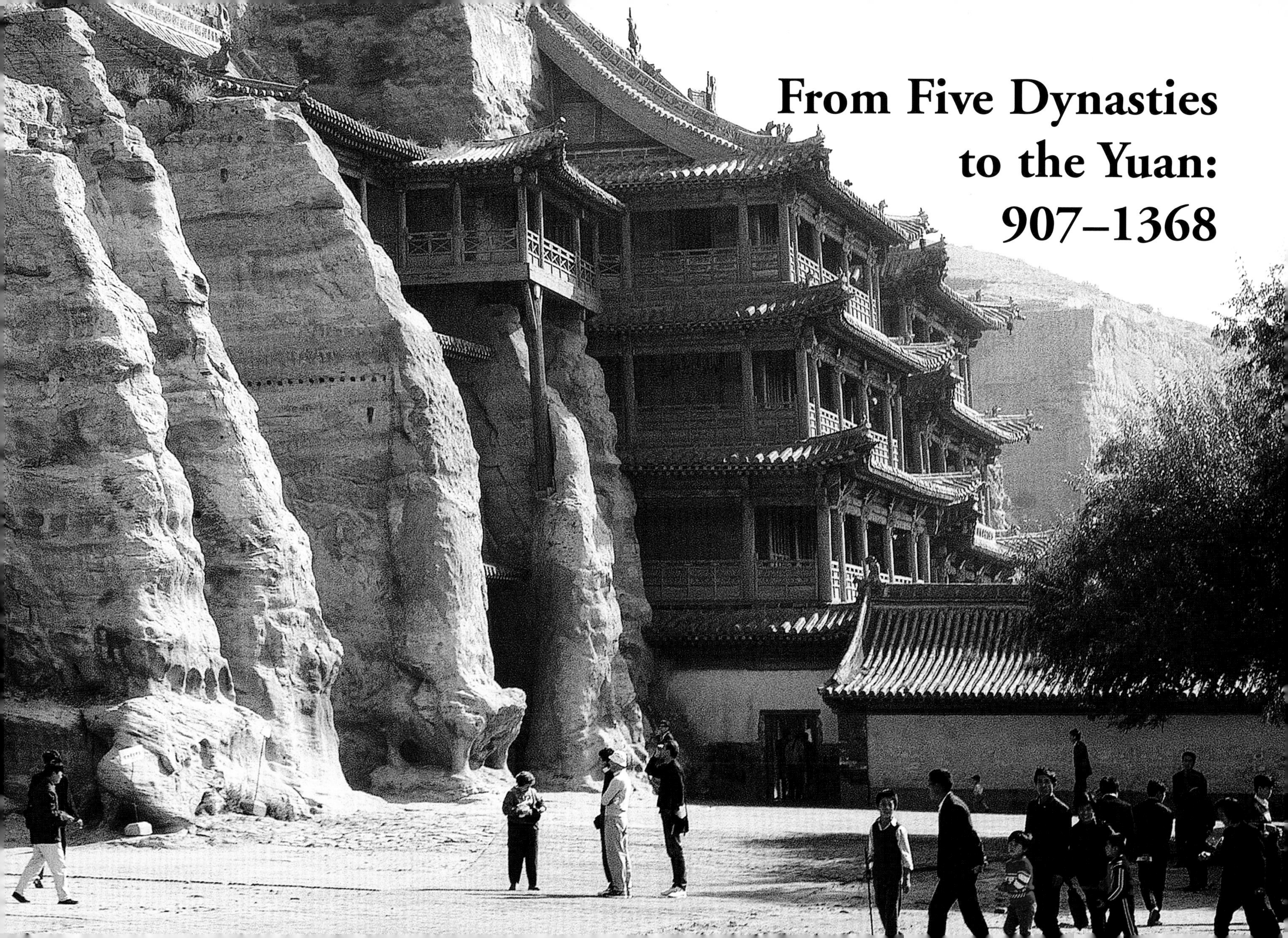

From Five Dynasties to the Yuan: 907–1368

The fall of the Tang Dynasty in 907 was followed by a period of disunity lasting some five decades that is aptly known as the Five Kingdoms and Ten Dynasties. The five kingdoms were the Later Liang (907–23), the Later Tang (923–936), the Later Jin (936–947), the later Han (947–950) and the later Zhou (951–960). A measure of unity was restored during the next dynasty, that of the Song. The Northern Song established their capital at Kaifeng from where they ruled a somewhat small empire. Their greatest problems were their neighbors. They managed to co-exist with the Liao, a non-Chinese dynasty that held an area of Chinese territory south of the Great Wall but faced much greater pressure in the northwest from another non-Chinese people, the Xi Xian.

The Northern Song empire actually fell to a previous ally, the non-Chinese Juchen, who took Kaifeng in 1126. The Juchen, who were the forebears of the Manchu, founded the Jin Dynasty with a capital near Beijing, while the Song fled southward to establish the Southern Song and make Hangzhou their new capital. The Song were forced to make regular tributes to the Jin in the form of silk, silver and tea. Despite these upheavals the Song Dynasty was one of great dynamism and much concrete achievement. The economy boomed with the production of rice soaring. This freed many people from working on the land and the empire saw the major expansion of many industries, such as silk manufacture, ceramics and mining. Trade was also expanded, especially with Southeast Asia and Japan, and both the arts and sciences flourished especially in the two capitals. Various petty restrictions enacted by the Tang were removed and ordinary people enjoyed greater freedoms.

Both the Jin and Song Dynasties were overwhelmed by the Mongols in the 13th century. Genghis Khan, who had been crowned Mongol emperor in 1206, took the lead, capturing Beijing in 1215. The Jin Dynasty finally ended in 1234 and the Southern Song lost Hangzhou in 1276, although they were not totally defeated until 1279. The grandson of Genghis, Kublai Khan, ruled over a vast empire as a member of the Yuan Dynasty (1206–1368). The Mongols and their non-Chinese allies dominated the empire, a fact that caused much growing resentment among the Chinese. This political faction-alism and major economic problems led to the outbreak of rebellion in northern and central China during the mid-14th century. The various rebel movements eventually coalesced around Zhu Yuangzhang and he established a new dynasty, the Ming, in 1368, thereby restoring Chinese rule.

PREVIOUS PAGE: In all, the Yungang caves comprise 252 grottoes, which contain over 50,000 small and large statues of Buddha. Made a UNESCO World Heritage Site in 2001, of particular interest are the Five Caves of Tan Yao. These superbly designed caves are considered the zenith of early Chinese art.

RIGHT: The largest and oldest of China's Taoist sculptures is in Quanzhou Province. Measuring over 15 feet high by 21 feet across, it depicts the father of Taoism, Lao Tzu, who is thought to have lived between the 6th and 4th centuries B.C., though this statue is only about 1,000 years old.

PAGE 70: Taken at Genghis Khan's 800th anniversary Festival of Eurasia, this photograph shows a re-enactment of a cavalry charge during the unification of the Mongolian tribes under Genghis Khan using 500 cavalrymen in the uniforms of the 13th century.

PAGE 71: This timeless Chinese scene shows a farmer outside Hangzhou in Zhejiang Province leading an ox across a footbridge. Such a sight would have been as common in China at the beginning of the second millennium with rice production reaching unprecedented levels.

RIGHT: Nomads herding horses on the Mongolian grasslands. Without the country's small but sturdy steeds, Genghis Khan would never have been able to conquer the largest empire in history. The Mongolian tactics were all based around the speed and stamina of their mounts—the "hit and run" raid being a favorite strategy.

FAR LEFT: The actual burial place of Genghis Khan is one of history's great mysteries; the Mausoleum of Genghis Khan in Inner Mongolia contains only an empty coffin. The building was constructed in the 1950s by the People's Republic of China to serve as a memorial to the great warrior. Located in the middle of the Ordos Grassland, the Genghis Khan Mausoleum contains a 15-foot statue of the Great Khan as well as friezes that commemorate his martial achievements.

LEFT AND RIGHT: This monument to Genghis Khan stands at Khodoo Aral in Mongolia, and marks the site of the first capital of the Mongolian Empire. Considered a national hero by the People's Republic of China, the Great Khan's contribution to Chinese history was considerable. It was his grandson Kublai Khan who founded the Yuan Dynasty in 1271 and brought the capital to Beijing.

FAR LEFT: Mount Tai is one of the five mountains sacred to Taoism in China as well as being a cradle of Chinese civilization. Of the many temples that adorn its slopes, perhaps the most influential is the Azure Cloud Temple, seen here. During the Ming Dynasty, the temple would have counted its annual visitors in the hundreds of thousands.

LEFT: Visitors to Mount Tai can climb the 7,200 steps to the East Peak passing 11 gates, 14 archways, 14 kiosks, and 4 pavilions. In all the mountain is also home to 22 temples, 97 ruins, and 819 carved stone tablets. The mountain has been a place of pilgrimage for over 3,000 years, but its history stretches back much further than this. Indeed, there is archeological evidence of human activity here going back 400,000 years.

ABOVE: Tourists enjoy the Wuyishan area in Fujian Province by boat. A region of outstanding natural beauty, Wuyishan was also an important Taoist site, centered on the Chongyou Wanniagong (Palace of Ten Thousand Years).

RIGHT: As elsewhere in the world, river traffic was vital to China's early development. Indeed, a glance at a map shows how many of China's major cities are located on the land's watery arteries. However, most run from west to east and empty into the Pacific. To remedy this, the Chinese spent over 1,700 years building the Grand Canal, which runs from north to south. An achievement on a par with the Great Wall, if not so widely known, construction on the world's longest and oldest man-made waterway began in 486 B.C.

ABOVE: A view of Yuantong Temple in Yuantong Park, Yunnan Province. The park has been the site of the important Buddhist temple since the Yuan Dynasty and is a superb example of Yuan and Ming architectural styles.

RIGHT: Known as the Iron Pagoda, this structure in Kaifeng in Henan Province is made of glazed bricks of red, brown, blue, and green. From a distance it appears reddish-brown, like rusted iron. Dating to 1049, the pagoda with its ornamental carvings has withstood almost 1,000 years of weathering and natural disasters.

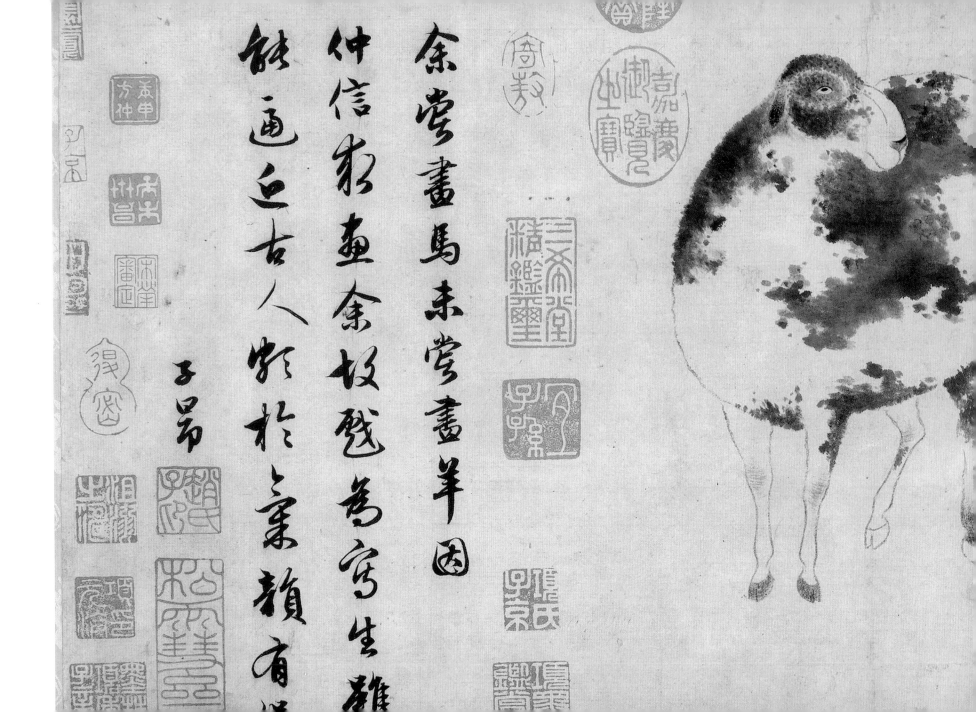

余嘗畫馬未嘗畫羊因
仲信求畫余故戲為寫生雖
不能逼近古人頗於氣韻有得
子昂

PAGES 82–83: A prince of the Song Dynasty, Zhao Mengfu (c. 1254–1322) was a high official, painter, and calligrapher who revolutionized Chinese art and is generally thought of as the founder of modern Chinese painting.

FAR LEFT: Scented smoke from a giant incense burner takes the prayers of the faithful to heaven at the Yuantong Temple. Built around an octagonal pavilion that is surrounded by water, the temple is set with extensive gardens.

LEFT: Dating to 977, the Fan Pagoda in Kaifeng is the oldest building in the city. When first constructed in the Song Dynasty, the pagoda would have had an additional six floors: these were removed during the Ming period then replaced by a smaller mini-pagoda in the Quing Dynasty. An important Buddhist site, displayed inside the pagoda are the poetry and writings of many of China's most famous literary figures.

The Ming Dynasty: 1368–1644

Built in 1420, the Temple of Heaven in Beijing was a place in which sacrifices were made to heaven. As the emperors feared to build their own palace bigger than the temple, it is slightly greater in size than the Forbidden City. This photograph shows the Hall of Prayer.

The Ming Dynasty: 1368–1644

The Ming Dynasty was founded by rebel leader Zhu Yuanzhang in 1368. He made Nanjing his capital, although it would be moved back to Beijing during the reign of Emperor Yongle in the early part of the 15th century. Zhu had been a harsh leader at a time when China needed a firm hand following the collapse of the Yuan Dynasty and Yongle, who ruled from 1403 to 1424, was an equally ruthless emperor. He seized power from his nephew, provoking a civil war that marred the early part of his reign. Yongle sought to regain favor and prestige by sending a eunuch general, Zheng He, at the head of a large fleet on seven expeditions to establish diplomatic and trading links. He also moved the capital back to Beijing, establishing the Forbidden City. The city also expanded beyond it original walls, especially its commercial and residential zones, and these were subsequently enclosed by a second wall in 1522, thus giving the city a layout that survived into the 1950s.

The 15th century also saw the Ming face other invaders; some peaceful, some less so. There was a dramatic incursion by the Mongols in 1439 and they held the emperor prisoner for 12 months. This trauma and the fear of further raids led them to extent the Great Wall by around 600 miles, but this could not prevent pirates raiding up and down the coast. During the middle of the

RIGHT: The Ming Tombs are a complex of mausoleums built around the magnificent Changling, the tomb of Emperor Zhu Di. Noted for their exquisite architecture, the tombs lie to the northwest of Beijing.

FAR RIGHT: A miniature painting depicting a hunting scene and the meeting of Marco Polo and Kublai Khan. Polo, together with his father and uncle, was one of the first Europeans to travel the Great Silk Road to Asia and became a favorite of Kublai Khan. He later wrote of his travels in 1298 when he found himself imprisoned in Genoa and furnished western historians with some of the earliest insights into Chinese culture.

il a bien .x. mille hommes entour luy. qui sont tuit ordonne. ij. et. ij. et saphel
lent tastaoz. qui vault a dire hommes qui se prennent garde. Car douze + douze
demenent ca du la. si que bien tiennent detoute asses.

century Europeans traders began arriving and the Portuguese were given the right to build a trading post at Macau in 1557.

The Ming Dynasty's undoing was a succession of weak rulers who left the running of the state to squabbling ministers and officials. This trend began in the reign of Zhu Houchao, who sat on the throne from 1505 to 1521 and intensified between 1621 and 1628 during the reign of Tianqi. He left the running of the country to a scheming eunuch, Wei Zhongxian. Periodic droughts and floods devastated much of northern China around this time and led to lawlessness and major unrest, but the country also faced other threats that came from beyond its borders.

The Jurchens were making frequent raids into China by the 1620s but these paled behind an invasion by the Manchu. They were originally halted by the Great Wall but were eventually let through by a Ming general, who hoped they would simply put down the rebellions that plagued the country and were closing in on Beijing. The capital fell to rebels under Li Zicheng in 1644 but he held the throne for a mere day before fleeing from Chinese troops who made a Manchu their new emperor thus establishing a new dynasty.

RIGHT: Serving as the Imperial Palace from the middle of the Ming Dynasty until the Qing Dynasty ended in 1911, the Forbidden City is one of the world's most famous buildings. Construction began in Beijing in 1406 under Zhu Di, the Yongle Emperor and was completed in just 14 years. It is believed that this great feat was made possible by the 200,000 workers who participated in the construction.

FAR RIGHT: The largest palace complex in the world, the buildings of the Forbidden city cover an area of 178 acres and are surrounded by a 30-foot wall as well as a wide moat.

PAGES 92–93: The name of the Forbidden City derives from the fact that the emperor's permission was needed for anyone to enter or leave the compound. Over the centuries that the palace was the center of political power in China it became a storehouse of treasure. An inventory taken in 1925 listed over 1.17 million items, including masterpieces of gold, silver, and jade as well as artworks and furniture.

PAGES 94–95: The last emperor of China, Puyi, who had been living in the palace since his abdication in 1912, was evicted in 1924, and since then the Chinese people have been careful to restore and maintain one of their great national treasures. The Forbidden City has been a protected building since 1961 and in 1987 became a UNESCO World Heritage Site.

ABOVE: The Temple of Heaven was begun in 1420 and became the empire's pre-eminent Taoist temple, visited by every emperor of the Ming and Qing dynasties after its completion.

FAR RIGHT AND RIGHT: The Hall of Prayer for Good Harvests is almost 100 foot in diameter yet was built without the use of a single nail. As with all of the structures in the complex it is roofed with blue tiles that symbolize heaven.

故宫博物院

LEFT: Imperial Masoleum of the Qing Dynasty in Shih-Huang-Ti.

ABOVE: The Forbidden City seen from Jingshan Park to the north. The park is a man-made hill landscaped from the spoil created by the construction of the moat around the Forbidden City.

RIGHT AND PAGES 102 AND 103: Pingyao in Shanxi Province is filled with excellent examples of ancient Chinese architecture, the foremost of which is the 40-mile-long wall that surrounds the city. Originally dating back to the 11th century B.C., the wall was rebuilt and enlarged during the Ming Dynasty. It is constructed of rammed earth faced with brick and stone and is topped with 72 watch towers. At 40 feet high along its length and 20 feet wide at the top, the wall is an impressive fortification.

LEFT: Construction of the first of the thirteen tombs of the Ming Dynasty began with the tomb of Zhu Di in 1409 and ended with the collapse of the dynasty in 1644. Over more than two centuries a fabulous necropolis was created, with each of the sumptuous mausoleums connected by the Sacred Road.

RIGHT: The village of Hongcun in Anhui Province is thought to be one of the best-preserved examples of Chinese village life in the medieval era and includes numerous Ming Dynasty dwellings.

ABOVE: The village of Hongcun was laid out in the shape of an ox to ensure good luck for its citizens and has been a UNESCO World Heritage Site since 2000. Hongcun is so redolent of medieval China that the village was selected as a location for filming the movie *Crouching Tiger, Hidden Dragon.*

RIGHT: In all Hongcun has around 150 residences, many of which were built during the Ming dynasty at a time when merchants from this region of China dominated Chinese trade.

LEFT: Having escaped the ravages of time and development due to its remote location, Hongcun now stands as testament to the customs and traditions of the past.

RIGHT: Hongcun's Chengzi Hall is a superb example of vernacular architecture. Within is a dwelling typical of the affluent village-dweller during this period, decorated with marble floors, black tiles, and red lanterns as well as some exquisite wood carvings.

The Qing Dynasty: 1644–1911

The Qing Dynasty: 1644–1911

The Manchu proclaimed the Qing Dynasty in 1644 but it took them some 40 years of often vicious campaigning to root out the last Ming supporters. As outsiders the Qing also sought to impose themselves on the wider population by taking care to include various other peoples in their administration but they also enacted harsh laws that outlawed the expression of anti-Manchu sentiments. The Qing also embarked on territorial expansion. Their own homeland, Manchuria, was incorporated into China proper, and Tibet, Xinjiang, and Taiwan all came under their control during the 18th century. The number of people ruled by them more than doubled between the founding of the dynasty and the close of the aforementioned century but not everyone accepted their rule and emperors had to suppress several rebellions.

Foreign traders initially from Portugal and Britain and Christian missionaries began to have a significant impact on China. They had been welcomed but this policy of openness to foreign commerce was reversed in the mid-18th Century when they were restricted to just one port, Guangzhou. The Chinese government also began to complain about the British trade in opium, which was causing untold misery among the wider Chinese population. Attempts to

PREVIOUS PAGE: A view over Hong Kong and Victoria Harbor to the Kowloon Peninsula. The island of Hong Kong was first occupied by the British in 1841 during the First Opium War.

RIGHT: A classic Chinese garden in Suzhou. From the 17th century onward, Europe became obsessed with all things Chinese.

Called Chinoiserie, everything from garden design to silks were exported to the west.

FAR RIGHT: The City of Peking as drawn by an unnamed European artist in 1858. At that time tensions between China and the western nations were becoming increasingly tense, and the city was stormed by and Anglo-French force during that year.

GENERAL VIEW OF THE CITY OF PEKIN, THE CAPITAL OF CHINA—NORTH SIDE.

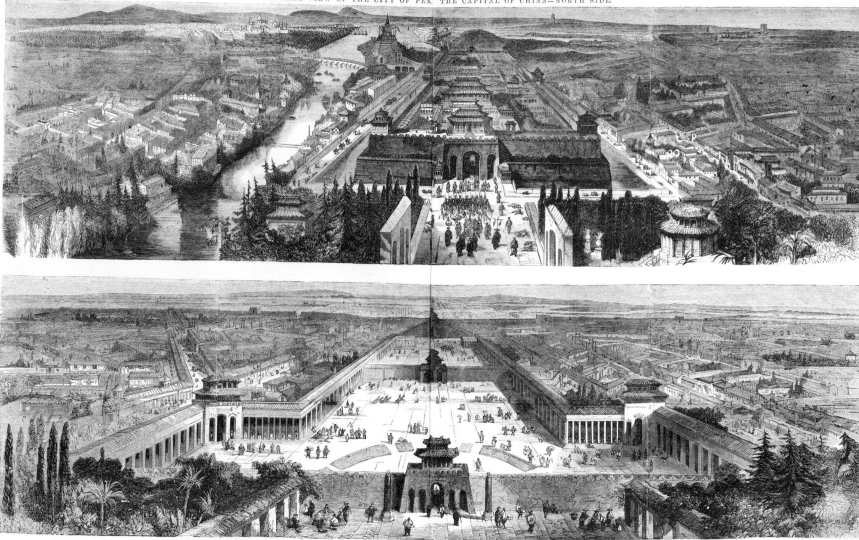

GENERAL VIEW OF THE CITY OF PEKIN—SOUTH SIDE.

PEKIN, THE CAPITAL OF CHINA.

THE new treaty just concluded between the United States and the Chinese Empire will probably enable us to have a Minister resident at Pekin. Hitherto, as every one knows, Pekin has been forbidden ground to barbarians. One or two embassies have penetrated its walls; but the embassadors have been compelled to travel in closed chairs, so that they saw very little more than they would have done had they been mere trunks—to which humble object one of the noblemen who made the journey compared himself. Now we shall soon know as much about Pekin as we know of Calcutta or Delhi. A few lines of history and description may prove an interesting preface to the books which threaten us with elaborate accounts of the Chinese capital.

Pekin, of course it is needless to say, is well known in China to have been founded many thousand years before the Christian era, and several thousand before the Creation and the Deluge. It seems to have been the principal political city in the empire at the time of the Tartar conquest; it was on the hill behind the palace which is seen in our illustration that the last Chinese monarch of the pure native dynasty cut his throat. On the dreadful night which witnessed the end of the sway of the Chinese Monarchs, the Tartar hills, fifteen miles distant, were red with the flames of the Imperial palace; the city, all built of brightly-painted wood, was a sea of fire; the convoy which conveyed the Tartar plunder to a place of safety was, it is said, thirty miles long.

Misfortunes fall heavy on Pekin. Scarce twenty years after the conflagration and the massacre which heralded the overthrow of the native dynasty, an earthquake overwhelmed the whole city, and buried 300,000 souls in the ruins. A few years afterward another like disaster cost Pekin 100,000 inhabitants. For the last two hundred years every generation has seen some riot or popular outburst which has been quenched in seas of blood.

To guard against riots no provision has been made by the Chinese law. Earthquakes are provided for by the laws respecting buildings. These laws forbid the construction of any edifice over one story high. Thus there is not a two-story house in all Pekin. The size and distribution of houses are likewise fixed by law. The size of every man's door is graduated according to his rank, and so is the architectural front of his house. A "common man" may not have columns before his door; a man of letters may have three rows; a mandarin five; a prince seven; the Emperor nine. So with the roof. The Emperor's roof is yellow, the princes' green, common citizens' blue or gray. Every thing is fixed by law, nothing is left to choice.

If the estimate which has been made of the population of Pekin—2,000,000 souls—be correct, nearly one twentieth of the whole number are independent of the laws concerning buildings, for they inhabit none. A hundred thousand people sleep every night in the streets, in the ruins, on the river, or halt the flow of opium into China led the British to launch two wars against the Chinese in the 1840s and 1850s and the former's victories in both paved the way for further exploitation of China by the other leading western powers of the day. They were joined by expansionist Japan after its forces had easily won a brief war in 1895 and Germany won trading concessions in 1898. Growing resentment against this foreign economic imperialism and the widespread proselytizing work of Christian missionaries led to an uprising, the Boxer Rebellion (1900–1901), that was eventually put down with considerable brutality by a multinational force.

By the beginning of the 20th century China was a weak and divided nation ruled over by an ineffective government headed by the Dowager Empress. She died in 1908 and the new emperor, Puyi (1906–1967), was a mere two years old and destined to be last Qing ruler. Unrest was never far below the surface and once again was based on foreign investment in the country, particularly its rail network. Opponents founded the Railway Protection Movement and it rapidly took on an anti-Qing dimension that was exploited by ardent nationalists. They wanted to create a wholly new state on the basis of the Three Principles of the People—nationalism, popular sovereignty, and livelihood. Unrest turned to rebellion in 1911 and the Nationalist quickly ousted Puyi, thus ending a dynasty that had ruled for more than 250 years.

RIGHT AND FAR RIGHT: **Suzhou in Jiangsu Province** can trace the history of its internationally famous gardens back almost 3,000 years. However, it was during the Qing Dynasty that landscape art reached its peak. Of the hundreds of breathtaking gardens that once flourished in the city, some still survive and are a monument to the ingenuity, sophistication, and artistry of the city's landscape designers.

RIGHT: The mountains of Wudang in Hubei Province are famous for the monasteries that can be found there. The first—Five Dragon Temple—was constructed during the Tang Dynasty, but building reached a peak during the Ming Dynasty.

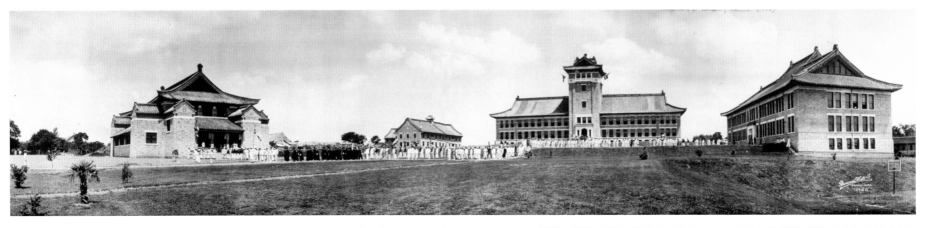

Taken by western photographers at the end of the 19th century, these photographs show Chinese scenes in the final years of the Qing Dynasty, before Imperial power was overthrown and China changed forever. Shown here are photos of Shanghai (LEFT), Nanjing (ABOVE), and the Great Wall (RIGHT).

FAR RIGHT: Shanghai at the end of the 19th century would have been a cosmopolitan city. Opened to international trade in the wake of the First Opium War, the boisterous city became home to migrants from across Europe and North America, who dubbed themselves "Shanghighlanders."

ABOVE, ABOVE RIGHT, AND RIGHT: Almost totally destroyed by the Anglo-French invasion force of 1860, then again during the Boxer Rebellion, Beijing's Summer Palace has been rebuilt on both occasions, though according to oral history its later incarnations have never quite matched the opulence and beauty of the first. The complex of palaces and gardens began as the Garden of Clear Ripples in 1750 (though an imperial garden has existed here sine the 12th century) and over the decades was expanded and landscaped into a massive compound of exquisitely manicured gardens, delicate pagodas and pavilions, boats, and bridges.

LEFT AND ABOVE: Lijiang City in Yunnan Province is a city of over a million with a rich history of eight centuries. Within its boundaries are the atmospheric old town district and four counties, which are home to such delights as the Jade Water Village, Tiger Leaping Gorge, and Lashi Lake.

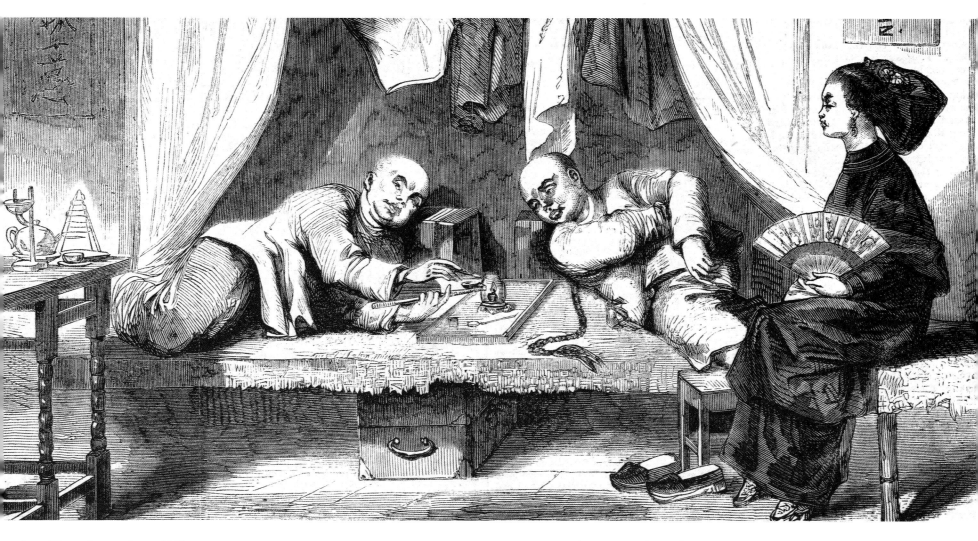

LEFT: The ancient rooftops of Lijiang, a UNESCO World Heritage Site since December 4, 1997. Famous for its system of waterways and bridges, it is often called the "Venice of the East."

ABOVE: A woman administers to the needs of two men as they smoke at an opium saloon in China. The British legalized opium smoking in China in 1858 and by 1900 more that 90 million people in that country were addicted. Attempts by the Chinese authorities to curb the import of the drug led to two wars with Britain and the eventual forced opening of the Chinese markets to the world.

LEFT AND RIGHT: This photograph of a street scene, taken around the beginning of the 20th century, illustrates town life around that time. The nation's long isolation from the west meant that new technologies were almost unheard of and life progressed much as it had for centuries. The photograph at right shows villagers processing tea.

LEFT: Allied French and English troops storm through a breech in the fortifications of Canton during the Tai Ping Rebellion of 1850–1864, a war begun by a Kwangsi district schoolmaster and mystic Hong Xiuquan, who believed himself the younger brother of Jesus Christ. Although the imperial forces were eventually victorious, the insurrection cost the lives of about 20 million. The Qing Dynasty was also fatally weakened and would fall within a few decades.

ABOVE LEFT, ABOVE RIGHT, AND PAGE 130: These three photographs were taken by western photographers accompanying interventionist troops during the Boxer Rebellion of 1899–1901. After years of western meddling in Chinese politics and trade and the country being held to unequal treaties, made under duress, the rebels attempted to expel foreign influence from China. In June 1900 Beijing was invaded and 230 foreigners were murdered. Elsewhere tens of thousands of Christian Chinese were also killed. Although the uprising was finally quelled with the help of the western powers, who also maintained the Imperial government following the rebellion, the days of the Qing Dynasty were numbered. The revolutionary movement gathered its strength over the next decade and in 1911, the Qing Dynasty was overthrown by the forces of Sun Yat-sen.

LEFT AND ABOVE: Boxer rebels on trial in the wake of the rebellion. The Boxer Protocol, which the Qing government was forced to sign with the allied western powers, called for the execution of ten court officials who had been connected to the rebels as well as many other lower-ranking officials. China was also fined a massive 333 million U.S. dollars in reparations, which was split between the eight allied nations who quelled the rebellion.

LEFT: This photograph is symbolic of the Qing Dynasty's submission to the west. It shows American troops marching within the walls of the Forbidden City during the Boxer Rebellion.

RIGHT: Sao Lourenco (St. Lawrence's) church in Macao was built in 1560 and was a jumping off point for Christian missionaries intent on converting China. A Portuguese colony until 1999, Macao was the first European colony in China and a busy center of trade.

LEFT AND FAR LEFT: A hundred miles northeast of Beijing is Chengde, the beautiful summer resort of the Qing emperors. Built during the 18th century, it is an ornate palace contained by high walls. Within the complex are parks and lakes dotted with pagodas.

LEFT: Originally taken by the British after the first of the opium wars, Hong Kong was returned to China shortly after. However, after the Second Opium War ended in 1860, the island became a permanent British colony along with Kowloon Peninsula and was declared a free port. Over the ensuing decades the city became a key trading point between east and west and its fortunes prospered.

LEFT: This view over Hong Kong and Victoria Harbor to the Kowloon Peninsula is undated, but the number and size of the buildings indicates that it was taken in the early 20th century. Note the heavy shipping in Victoria Harbor: Hong Kong was an extremely busy port.

ABOVE: Hong Kong in the mid-19th century. Although the island formally belonged to the Chinese at this time, the British colony of Victoria City remained on the island and prospered.

BELOW: By the end of the 19th century, Hong Kong boasted large and elaborate buildings in the European style, such as the Harbor Building shown here. These would have been the headquarters of busy trading companies.

RIGHT: Hong Kong was finally restored to the Chinese in 1997, but its success as a port and the limited space available there had paved the way to it becoming a city of modern skyscrapers by the late 20th century. Shown here is the island's tallest building, Two International Finance Centre, which was completed in 2003.

FAR RIGHT: Hong Kong's distinctive double-decker trams have been in operation since 1904 and are still used by up to a quarter of a million commuters each day.

Modern China: 1911 to the Present

Development of the Pudong New Area in
Shanghai began in 1990 and it has since
become the heart of finance and commerce
in China. The area's imaginative skyline
includes the unique Oriental Pearl Tower,
which is punctuated with spheres.

Modern China: 1911 to the Present

By any measure modern China had a traumatic birth. After the fall of the last emperor in 1911, the Republic of China was founded by Sun Yat-sen but almost immediately the Provisional Republican Government fell apart. The man who had forced the abdication of the last emperor, Yuan Shikai, was made president but in 1915 declared that he was the country's new emperor. Although Yuan died shortly thereafter, several provinces effectively broke away from China and had become the fiefdoms of various warlords by the end of the 1920s. What remained of China was also rent by political divisions, chiefly between the nationalist Kuomintang and the Chinese Communist Party. They were uneasy bedfellows at the best of time but relations worsened in the late 1920s.

The Nationalists under Chiang Kaishek attempted to spread their influence farther afield by taking on the warlords and then the communists. Resistance to Chiang Kaishek coalesced around Mao Zedong who advocated a rural-based communist revolt, but he had to lead his forces on the Long March in 1934–1935 to avoid complete destruction at the hands of the Nationalists. The aggressive and expansionist military regime in Japan took advantage of this upheaval. Its troops occupied Manchuria in 1931 and

RIGHT: Another of Pudong's impressive skyscrapers is the Jin Mao Tower. This photograph is of the balconies in the atrium looking down from the Grand Hyatt Hotel which starts on the 57th floor of the building.

FAR RIGHT: For many years Macao was a seaport notorious for its licentiousness. Since it was returned to China by the Portuguese in 1999, its gambling traditions have continued unabated. This photograph shows the Sands Casino.

invaded China itself in 1937. Both the Nationalists and communists fought the invaders but it was the latter who also took the opportunity to spread their influence as never before.

The end of World War II did not end China's misery as civil war broke out 1946. The turning point came after the communists won three great battles in Manchuria, and Mao was able to proclaim the foundation of the People's Republic of China on October 1, 1949. Mao ruled China until his death in 1976 and the country was run along strictly communist lines. Although in many respects the lives of ordinary people generally improved, their personal freedom was limited as dissent was not tolerated in any form.

China began to change dramatically in the latter part of the 20th century. The country remained tightly supervised with regard to personal freedoms but many of the restraints on what had been a state-controlled economy were effectively removed.

Today's China is likely to become the world's leading economy in the not too distant future, but this very success has brought its own problems. The main concern is that the economic miracle has not filtered down to the lower echelons of its society, chiefly the rural poor who constitute the vast majority of the population, and this wealth imbalance has already begun to cause considerable social disruption. Equally, those who are enjoying the fruits of the economic boom may begin demanding the greater personal freedoms that the regime has so far denied them.

PAGES 148–149: The Bund, in Shanghai, is an historic road lined with buildings that recall the city's colonial past and importance as a banking and trading hub. Today, it is promoted as a tourist destination by the Shanghai government while, with the recent relaxation of China's economic policies, many of the old buildings have once again become the premises of western banks and businesses.

RIGHT: A laborer takes a rest during construction work on the Three Gorges Dam. The largest hydroelectric dam in the world, it was completed in 2006.

FAR RIGHT: Jiuzhaigou Valley means Valley of Nine Villages—but few of the original Tibetan villages survive today. The main feature of the area is its karst topography and its brightly colored lakes.

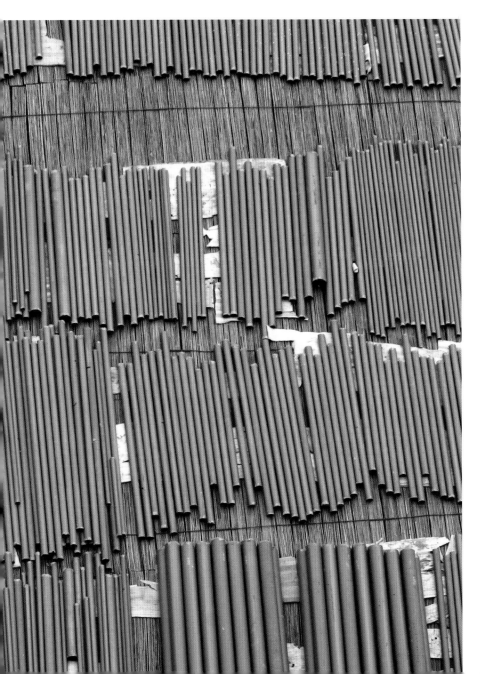

ABOVE: Seen during record low water levels caused by drought, the Yangtze River has been culturally and economically important to the Chinese since the earliest times. Home to a number of rare species, including the Finless Porpoise, the river has been polluted by the industries that have grown up on its banks and there are fears that, like the Yangtze River Dolphin, more of the Yangtze's unique wildlife may become extinct.

RIGHT: A coal power plant in Hebei Province. China's rapid economic growth has been powered by fossil fuels, which has raised grave environmental concerns and made several of the nation's cities among the most polluted in the world. In response the government has made a commitment to cleaner energy sources under the Law on Renewable Energy of 2006, which aims to provide 10 percent of the country's electricity needs from renewable energy by 2010. With its burgeoning economy, there is hope that China may become a world leader in ecologically friendly power.

LEFT: While the Cultural Revolution of 1966 did much to undermine the traditional Chinese way of life, today's government is keen to embrace the past. The achievements and culture of pre-revolutionary China are seen as integral elements in the make up of the national identity.

RIGHT AND PAGE 154: Since the late 1970s, China has been moving away from a typically centralized Communist economy and embraced the world markets, though government control is still rigid. For China's people this has meant that personal income has risen and consumerism is now actively encouraged as can be seen in busy malls and markets in the country's towns and cities.

PAGE 155: At the time of publication, Beijing is undergoing a facelift in time for the 2008 Olympics, which the city will host. The massive construction project has come at a cost though: some 300,000 homes have been demolished and their occupants relocated.

LEFT: The highest mountain in the world, Mount Everest stands on the border of Chinese-controlled Tibet and Nepal.

RIGHT: A deeply Buddhist country, Tibet's traditional head of state was the Dalai Lama until China took control of the country in 1959. This pagoda (called a chorten in Tibet, meaning funeral pyre) is a Buddhist structure that was built to contain a relic or sutra (collection of recorded Buddhist dialogues and discourses).

LEFT: The Potala Palace was once the residence of the Dalai Lama and is now a state museum. While China has assured a degree of autonomy in Tibet, there are loud calls—led by the Dalai Lama—for genuine self-government. A matter of international concern, it does not look likely that Tibet will become free of China in the near future.

RIGHT AND FAR RIGHT: Tibet is located on the high plateau, and most of the Himalaya range lies within the country. It is also the source for many of the greatest rivers of Asia: the Brahmaputra, Ganges, Indus, Mekong, Yangtze, and Yellow.

Photo Credits
Map page 13 courtesy Mark Franklin.
Via Jo St Mart: 2 Bjorn Svensson; 8, 25, 28, 30, 31, 33, 34–35, 36, 61, 62, 66, 91, 92–93, 94–95, 134, 135 China National Tourism; 12, 100 Suichu Ru; 14 (both), 16, 20 (both), 21, 23R, 24, 29, 38, 39, 43L, 44, 48, 55, 57, 59 (both), 64, 65 (both) 152, 153, 154, 156, 157, 158, 159 (both) Shutterstock; 17, 41, 45, 58, 60, 97L, 98, 99, 102, 107, 108, 124 photolibrary.com; 18, 32 Herbert Hopfensperger; 22, 136, 141 (both) Philip Allport; 42, 43R Sylvain Grandadam; 46, 116 Wojtek Buss; 47 Luis Casta; 50 Krause & Johansen; 51 Fuste Raga; 52 Weixiong Liu; 53 Panorama; 56 Dennis Cox; 76 Bruno Perousse; 77 Zhou Jun; 79, 105, 106, 147 Panorama Media (Beijing) Ltd. / Alamy; 86–87 Wxeixiong Liu; 103 Bruce Bi; 109 Juan Carlos; 121L Ioseba Egibar
Library of Congress: 118 (all), 119, 129 (both), 130, 131R
Corbis: 4–5 Underwood & Underwood; 10 Nir Elias/Reuters; 19, 54 Jose Fuste Raga; 23L Julia Waterlow, Eye Ubiquitous; 69, 74, 151 Liu Liqun; 70, 72–73 Barry Lewis; 71 Yang Liu; 75 (both) Michel Setboun; 80, 84 Brian A. Vikander; 81 Lowell Georgia; 82–83 Smithsonian Institution; 85 Demetrio Carrasco/JAI; 89 Archivo Iconografico, SA; 110–111 Robert Landau; 113 Corbis; 125 Corbis; 126, 127, 131L Hulton-Deutsch Collection; 128 Corbis; 132, 138 Bettmann; 133 Yang Liu; 139 Albright-Knox Art Gallery; 140 Michael Maslan Historic Photographs; 142–143, 148 Bob Krist; 144 Jose Fuste Raga; 145 Yang Liu; 146 Reuters; 150 Qiu Shafeng/epa; 155 Jose Fuste Raga
Getty Images: 6–7 Jerry Driendl; 26–27 Gavin Hellier; 37, 38 National Geographic; 63 National Geographic; 120 Walter Bibikow/Taxi